Healthy Options!

Vegetarian Menu Plans And Recipes
With Daily Shopping Lists!

By Chef Linda Trubey

Go Light Your World And Pass It On!

Medical Disclaimer:
The health information in this book is based on my own
experience and research. Because each person and situation
are unique, the reader should check with a qualified
professional regarding their health care.

ISBN-13 : 978-1463786625
ISBN-10 : 146378662X

Healthy Options Catering
327 Colony Lane
Hendersonville, NC 28791

828.891.7529

Table of Contents

DEDICATION

I dedicate this book to God who has led me out of darkness into His beautiful light. "You shall know the truth, and it shall set you free."

ACKNOWLEDGMENTS

I thank my family for their support and love which have allowed me to share my story with you. My children and grandchildren include; Anne, April, Cari, Brandee, Aurora, Kevin, Rachel, Alyssa, Savannah, Haley, Kaylah, Brooklin, Zackery, and Ysabella.

Daniel Trubey, I believe God brought us together for a reason and I am so glad that He did. I love and appreciate you and your children; Shelley, Greg, Cameron, Ellie, Camille, Shawn, Camden, Acadia, Garrett, and Jenny, each day. I am so grateful for my extended family and I love each one of you!

Tracy,
So Great to
Meet you at True You
Climb! Best Wishes on your
Marathon,

Love, Linda

About The Author

Linda Trubey lives in Hendersonville North Carolina with her husband, Daniel, and her personal trainer, Raymond, their Lab-Rott. mix dog. She is the owner and head chef at Healthy Options Catering. Linda teaches Chef Classes from her home and at different locations around the world. If you would like to attend a live training class or invite Linda to speak and demonstrate some of her recipes for your group please contact her at www.ChefLindaTrubey.com

Introduction

I began my journey to improved health in 2005, after rediscovering the wonderful benefits of fresh fruits and vegetables. I learned to replace dairy with healthy substitutes.

The results were awesome and fast. I lost over 30 lbs. and lowered my blood pressure naturally. My allergies completely disappeared and my eyesight improved. Now I want to share my story and some of my favorite recipes with you in this book.

Do you come home from a long day and wonder what to eat? Are you confused about how to prepare delicious and healthy meals for you and your family? You need to have a plan.

Planning ahead will save you time, stress, and money.

Part 1.   My Story

My story begins on the day my husband, Al Dunlop, came home from a doctor appointment with the news that he had pancreatic cancer.

He had not been feeling well and he had lost about 50 lbs., just a few months ago, his doctor had diagnosed him as being diabetic and started him on medication to control his diabetes.

Now he was telling me he had an appointment with a cancer specialist in three days! **We were both in shock and did not want to believe this terrible news.**

I went with Al to speak with the cancer specialist. As we waited for our turn to see the doctor, we noticed many people with hats and scarves on to cover their balding heads; a side effect of chemo therapy. What did our future hold?

The doctor told us Al's cancer was growing fast and had already spread to his liver, kidney, stomach, and spleen. The doctor told us Al had stage 4 pancreatic cancer with only 1-3 months left to live.

 Al was only 56 years old. We had been married almost 23 years and I could not imagine my life without him.

God sees the future and He knows what is best for each of us. He does not prevent bad things from happening, but he does promise to never leave us. He goes through the storms of life with us. God gave us a peace that passes understanding.

www.ChefLindaTrubey.com

A friend from Oregon told me about Hallelujah Acres, a Christian ministry that provides education and resources to help people understand and practice God's ways to ultimate health.

I went to their website at hacres.com and read many stories of healing from all kinds of diseases by eating raw food and drinking fresh carrot juice. The stories were encouraging. It made so much sense to me that we need to eat fresh fruits and vegetables for our health.

I began to juice carrots and the juice helped us both to feel better and have more energy. As Al's cancer grew, it became hard for him to keep food down. The juice from the carrots and celery were easy for him to digest because they were in liquid form. He was able to take small sips throughout the day and it gave him some concentrated nutrition.

George Malkmus, the founder of Hallelujah Acres, was diagnosed with colon cancer and was not expected to live much longer. He began a search for a cure and discovered the powerful effects of raw foods and vegetable juices. He is now cancer free and has more energy than most people his age.

A few years later, I visited Hallelujah Acres main headquarters in Shelby, NC. I took a 12 week course, Get Healthy/Stay Balanced, which focuses on God's natural health laws; Nutrition, Exercise, Water, Sunshine, Temperance, Fresh Air, Rest, and Trust in God.

When you follow these health principles you will experience a more abundant life. Learn and practice these principles then pass them on to others. Go light your world.

My background is in food service and nursing. I worked for the local Home Health and Hospice Agency in Coldwater, Michigan; before we opened our home as a state licensed adult foster care home.

God blessed our efforts as we moved forward with our plans to open our AFC Home. I called the nearby nursing home to ask about purchasing used hospital beds. They told me they had just received a grant for all new beds and they would be putting their old beds and mattresses out by their dumpster in 1 week.

They were not permitted to sell the beds, however, they told me to come by and help myself at no charge. We picked up six beds with mattresses and two night stands. What a blessing!

Our first resident was a man from our church. His wife had just died and he was living at the nursing home. He was so happy to move in with us. It gave us a good income and saved him a couple of hundred dollars per month, so we were both happy.

Another AFC Home in our town decided to close and we received two more residents. Two ladies who wanted to stay together and be roommates. They were so excited that they found a room to share at our home. They told me I was an answer to their prayers and I told them they were an answer to my prayer. God has a plan for each one of us.

When Al was no longer able to work because of his pain from the cancer, I was able to care for him at home. God sent two more residents to cover our expenses at just the right time.

We called Hospice and they sent nurses to our home who were so kind and helpful. I had worked for this Hospice agency so I knew the nurses well.

Making a video scrapbook

Al and I watched our home videos and chose memories of vacations, weddings, births, and parties to make a video scrapbook for our family. Al and I shared our testimony and our love and faith in God on this video.

Our goal is to go to heaven and to have our family members with us. We do not deserve to go there, but Jesus died to save us from our sins. We can trust in Him to keep His promises.

This world is not going to last much longer. Someday soon Jesus will return to take those who love Him to live with Him throughout eternity.

It makes me sad that some people choose not to go to heaven. We are valuable children of God and are precious in His sight.

If we confess our sins, God is faithful and just to forgive us and to cleanse us from all unrighteousness. Just ask and you will receive. Seek God and you will find Him. It is not easy but God is there to help and to guide you one step at a time.

Looking forward to heaven takes some of the sting from death. Our death on this earth does not need to be a final death. Jesus is coming again to take those who love Him to live with Him.

Al was able to hold his new granddaughter and to spend time with all our family members before he died. He died quietly at home surrounded by family. Hospice nurses had kept him comfortable with pain medications.

My Pastor and some ladies from my church helped to organize Al's funeral service. We played the video scrapbook we had put together; celebrating all the fun times we had together as a family.

The service was a celebration of a life well lived and a man well loved by all who knew him.

We passed out small candles and lit them from a large candle in front of Al's picture, representing him sharing his light with us. "Pass It On" and "Go Light Your World" were sung by some friends of mine.

The words to those songs are so very meaningful to me and can be found at the end of this book.

After Al's death, a real identity crisis hit me. I was used to being half of a couple. Now I was a widow. What did I want to do with the rest of my life?

A friend suggested I make a "memory box" to keep cards, letters, and special photos; so I would have a place to go when I needed to feel a connection and remember the love that we shared. This is a great idea and I have shared it with others.

My adult foster care home allowed me to continue to work from home. Christian programs helped me to keep my focus on God and the blessings all around me. I am thankful for my children and my grandchildren.

Time for a change

My health was a concern to me because I was overweight and I had high blood pressure. I was worried that a hospital stay would wipe out my savings because I did not have medical insurance.

I knew I needed to make some changes for my health, so when I read about a "Eat And Be Well" class starting in January, I decided to join the class to support my decision to get healthy.

I learned about the importance of dark green leafy vegetables to our health. They are a rich source of vitamins and minerals and help to balance our PH. Greens are alkaline and help to prevent disease, which grows in an acidic environment.

If we become too acidic our body will pull calcium from our bones, which weakens them, in an attempt to balance our PH, to keep us alive.

I started eating more green lettuce, kale, and collards. I learned about making fruit green smoothies and the health benefits I received from drinking them were amazing.

I noticed a change right away. My body began to cleanse and to heal itself. My extra weight melted off my body. I went from a size 18 to a size 8.

My energy went through the roof!

I looked and felt 10 years younger. My blood pressure returned to normal and I was able to discontinue my medications.

My allergies disappeared completely. I felt empowered by taking response ability for my own health.

My family and friends noticed a change in my appearance and in my attitude. They wanted to learn what my secret was.

It really is simple and getting back to basics. We make it more complicated than it needs to be, because of our addiction to chemically laden foods. A piece of fruit is the ultimate fast food and best for you eaten fresh from the garden.

Cooking food over 118 degrees destroys the live enzymes and most of the vitamins and minerals the fresh food contains.

When we eat live food the digestive enzymes it contains are available to assist us in the digestion of that food. When we eat a lot of cooked and processed food our metabolic enzymes are called to help us digest our food and we lose energy and become tired.

Slowly your tastes will change to crave that which is good for you. Just start adding more fresh fruits and fresh vegetables to your meals and notice the extra energy you will have.

Support is an important key to your success. Surround yourself with others who want to get healthy and encourage each other.

When I hold a series of classes we assign each person a "Success Buddy" for accountability and support. There are online support groups as well.

Living On Live Food Chef Training

I bought Alissa Cohen's book, Living On Live Food. When I learned that Alissa was holding chef training classes; I traveled to Kittery, Maine, to be trained by Alissa and become a Certified Living On Live Food Chef Teacher through her program.

It was an amazing experience for me to spend a week with Alissa and 24 other students learning and absorbing the positive energy all around us. The recipes were easy to make and they tasted delicious! It helped to watch Alissa prepare her recipes and it gave me the confidence that I could do the same.

When I got back home I decided to close my AFC Home and to teach Raw Food Chef Classes.

I signed up for a Certified Natural Health Practitioner Course from the University of Natural Health. I wanted to learn as much as I could about natural cures for diseases.

I do believe many diseases can be prevented by our lifestyle choices. When I was depressed I did not feel like exercising. When I started making better food choices, I felt more energy and I actually wanted to exercise.

I enjoy showing others how easy it is to prepare healthy and delicious meals. I think it helps to see it being made and to taste the results for yourself, that is why I like to do live demonstrations during my classes.

Move to North Carolina

I met a wonderful Christian man, Daniel Trubey, we dated for a year and then we married on the same day we met a year later. God blessed us both by bringing us together. Our love for God has bonded us together from our hearts.

I moved to North Carolina with Daniel. I felt a little like Job; remember his story in the Bible? His faith was tested and he lost his family. Then God restored double to him for remaining faithful. Daniel is the father to four wonderful adult and married children. By marrying him, my family more than doubled in size!

The joy of the Lord is our strength.

When we step out for God our faith is tested. The devil does not want us to share our faith and he will do whatever he can to discourage us. We are not an effective witness for God if we are a mad or a sad Christian. The devil wants to steal our joy.

When I scheduled a Raw Food Class at my church, I became ill and went to the hospital ER. I had a kidney stone and when the doctor removed the stone, my body went into septic shock.

Ten days later, I woke up in ICU and was told that I had almost died. I had been put on a respirator, a feeding tube, and 3 IV bags with different medications to try to keep me alive.

My family came to see me and I was unresponsive. My daughter took a couple of pictures while I was in the ICU and I am glad she did. It was hard for me to believe that I was in there for 10 whole days!

Later, a memory came back to me. I heard a machine beeping and I was struggling to breathe. **I felt that I was on the verge of death**. It was tempting to just relax and go to sleep until Jesus would come to take me home.

I saw Dan, my husband of three months, standing near my bed and looking very worried. I wanted to spend more time with him and not make him go to my funeral just yet, so I made the decision to fight to live.

There is power in making a decision!

I am here today because of the choices I have made in my past. **You are where you are today because of your past choices. Your future is up to you and the decisions you make each day.**

Where do you want to be in your life one year from today? How about five years from today? Where do you want to be? Do you have a plan to get you there?

Your journey to improved health can start today.

The first step is to decide you want to take control of your own health. Then add some fresh romaine lettuce and leafy greens to each meal. Try a fruit smoothie using fresh fruit and add a handful of spinach or kale to the smoothie. When it is blended it will taste delicious. Add a frozen banana to make it cold and creamy. This is a very easy and delicious way to start your day.

You will find menus and recipes in this book to help you. Slowly your body will cleanse and your taste will change to enjoy and crave that which is good for you.

Our body knows what we need and will thank us for treating it with the love and respect it deserves. When we listen to what our body is trying to tell us we will crave that vitamin or mineral our body needs.

We are fearfully and wonderfully made in the image of God.

The Bible says we are transformed by the renewing of our mind. I encourage you to keep learning and experimenting to become empowered to take response ability for your own health. It becomes easier as you make one healthy choice at a time.

In my life I have made some good choices and some bad choices. Each decision has its own consequences, sometimes others are hurt and sometimes they are blessed by my choices.

Romans 12:1, 2 God pleads with us to offer our body as a living sacrifice, which is our act of worship. To no longer conform to the patterns of this world, but to be transformed by the renewing of our mind, so we can know God's perfect will for us.

There will always be trials and troubles in our life on this earth. People do not always make the right choices. God is preparing a place for us where there will be no more pain or sorrow. He desires each one of us to live with Him for eternity. I want to be there with my family and friends.
I hope you will be there also.

Part 2

Healthy Option Menus

15

www.ChefLindaTrubey.com

HEALTHY OPTION MENUS

(B)reakfast (L)unch (D)inner (S)nack

B- Easy No Bake Granola* + Almond Milk*+ Banana
L- Tofu Fried Rice* + Oriental Salad*+ Dressing*
D- Organic Garden Minestrone Soup* + Garlic Toast
S- Sliced Apples + Almond Butter or Raw Nuts

B- Fruit Green Smoothie* + Scrambled Tofu Wrap*
L- Vegetable Lasagna*+ Garlic Bread + Romaine Salad
D- Vegetable Sub Sandwiches + Vegetable Sticks + Dip
S- Healthy Options Apple Crisp* + Banana Cream*

B- Oatmeal + Banana + Walnuts + Dates
L- Harvest Nut Roast* + Baked Potatoes + Broccoli
D- Chick-Pea Noodle Soup* + Fresh Fruit Salad
S- Roasted Red Pepper Humus* + Baby Carrots

.

*Note: The recipes are included for the * items.

HEALTHY OPTION MENUS

B- Oatmeal Waffles* + Berry Sauce* + Cashew Whip*
L- Nut Meat Balls* BBQ Sauce*+ Baked Potato + Peas
D- Black Bean Burgers* + Buns + Potato Wedges*
S- Healthy Options Carmel Corn* + Apple Slices

B- Scrambled Tofu Breakfast Wrap *+ Salsa
L- Pecan-Oat Burgers* + Corn + Tossed Salad
D- Vegan Chick'n Pot Pie* + Quick Crust*+ Fruit
S- Trail Mix, Nuts, Raisins, Seeds, Dried Fruit

B- Whole Grain Toast + Peanut Butter + Applesauce
L- Shepherd Pie*+ Vegan Gravy* + Sweet Kale Salad*
D- Baked Macaroni and Cashew Cheese* + Fruit Salad
S- Frozen Fruit Smoothie* + Granola Bar

B- Breakfast Banana Split* + Cashew Whip *+ Nuts
L- Bean Enchiladas* + Spanish Rice* + Salsa + Chips
D- Black Bean Soup* + Whole Grain Dinner Rolls
S- Vegetable Sticks + Spicy Bean Dip or Humus*

*Note: The recipes are included for the * items.

HEALTHY OPTION MENUS

B- Three Grain Cereal *+ Orange Slices + Dates
L- Nut-Meat Balls *+ Gravy* + Mashed Potatoes + Carrots
D- Three Bean Chili *+ Corn Chips + Tofu Sour Cream*
S- Healthy Options Carmel Corn*+ Sliced Apples

B- All you can eat Cantaloupe and Watermelon Slices
L-Spanish Rice*or Stuffed Green Peppers + Bean Salad
D- Fettuccine with Creamy Pesto Sauce* + Tossed Salad
S- Peachy Cobbler* + Banana Whipped Cream*

B- Granola* + Almond Milk* + Grapefruit or Orange
L- Mock Chicken Salad* + Vegetable Sticks +Ranch Dip*
D- Eggplant Parmesan* + Romaine Salad + Italian Dressing*
S- Carob Fudge* + Sliced Oranges

*Note: The recipes are included for the * items.

Part 3

Healthy Option Recipes

DAY 1 RECIPES

Easy No Bake Granola

2 C. Rolled Oats

2 C. Quick Oats

¼ C. Millet, Ground

¼ C. Honey

½ tsp. Vanilla

¼ C. Pumpkin Seeds

¼ C. Shredded Coconut

1 tsp. Cinnamon (optional)

¼ C. Apple Juice Concentrate

½ tsp. Sea Salt

¼ C. Sunflower Seeds

¼ C. Dried Cranberries

Combine dry ingredients. In a separate bowl, mix wet ingredients then add to oat mixture and mix well. Place in airtight glass container and refrigerate. Use as a topping, a snack or as cereal.

Almond Milk

1/2 C. Raw Almonds, soaked

½ tsp. Vanilla Extract

2 C. Water

¼ tsp. Sea Salt

Place ingredients into blender and blend well. You can add more water until desired taste. A frozen banana will make it cold and creamy. If you like it sweet you can add dates or honey. For a different flavor try cashews or sesame seeds in place of the almonds.

Tofu Fried Rice

4 C. Brown Rice, cooked

1 lb. Organic Tofu, Firm

2 T. Soy Sauce + 3 T. Water

¼ C. Peanut or Almond Butter

2 Cloves Garlic, minced

½ T. Onion Powder

2 C. Celery, sliced

1 C. Green Pepper

1 C. Broccoli Florets

1 C. Onions, sliced

½ C. Green Onions

½ C. Carrots, sliced

Squeeze rinsed tofu dry and cut into small cubes. Make a sauce by mixing soy sauce, water, peanut butter, garlic, and onion powder together then marinate tofu and bake at 350 degrees for 5-10 minutes. Steam sliced vegetables in small amount of water. Add brown rice and tofu then bake until warm. Top with sliced almonds and green onion slices. This is great in a whole grain tortilla wrap!

Oriental Salad

1 Head Cabbage, chopped

2 Carrots, shredded

4 Green Onions sliced

1 C. Sliced Almonds

¼ C. Sesame Seeds

1 C. Chow Mein Noodles

Toast the almonds and noodles then add the sesame seeds. Allow to cool. Combine cabbage, carrots, green onions, and noodle mixture in a large bowl. You can substitute green lettuce chopped fine in place of the cabbage.

Oriental Salad Dressing

¼ C. Sesame Oil   ½ tsp. Ground Ginger
¼ C. Olive Oil   1 tsp. Sea Salt
¼ C. Honey   ½ tsp. Cayenne Pepper
¼ C. Lemon Juice   2 T. Sesame Seeds, toasted

Combine ingredients in a jar with a tight fitting lid and shake well then refrigerate. Add dressing just before serving salad.

Organic Garden Minestrone Soup

¼ C. Olive Oil   2 Cloves Garlic, minced
½ C. Carrots, shredded   1 C. Onion, minced
4 C. Vegetable Broth   2 T. Fresh Parsley, minced
½ C. Zucchini, chopped   2 C. Red Kidney Beans
1 tsp. Oregano   ½ C. Italian Green Beans
2 C. Small White Beans   1 tsp. Basil
¼ C. Celery, minced   2 C. Diced Tomatoes
¼ tsp. Thyme   3 C. Hot Water
3 C. Baby Spinach   ½ C. Small Shell Pasta

Sauté onion, celery, garlic, green beans, and zucchini in the oil for 5 minutes then add broth and other ingredients except spinach and pasta and simmer for 30 minutes then add spinach and pasta and cook for 5-10 more minutes.

DAY 2 RECIPES

Fruit Green Smoothie

1 C. Water	1 C. Frozen Fruit (Banana)
1 Apple, cored	2 C. Spinach or Kale
1 C. Pineapple	¼ C. Parsley or Cilantro

Put all ingredients into a blender and whirl up a smoothie. You can use any kind of fruit or frozen fruit. Apples mix well with greens and provide pectin. Frozen bananas add a creamy and cold texture. Experiment to find a flavor you like.

Scrambled Tofu Breakfast Wrap

1 lb. Tofu	½ C. Green Onions, sliced
¼ C. Nutritional Yeast	1 C. Potatoes, cooked & diced
2 tsp. Chick Seasoning	¼ C. Green Bell Pepper
¼ tsp. Garlic Powder	¼ C. Water
½ tsp. Turmeric	½ C. Non-Dairy Cheese

Sauté green onions in the water until the water is evaporated then stir in seasoned tofu and simmer for 10 minutes. Add remaining ingredients and heat well. Serve in whole grain flour tortillas with your favorite toppings; salsa, olives, guacamole, baco bits, or sausage-style crumbles.

www.ChefLindaTrubey.com

Vegetable Lasagna

1 Onion, sliced
1 Recipe of Tofu Cheese
1 C. Spinach, cooked
2 T. Olive Oil
1 (26 oz.) Pasta Sauce
2 T. Parsley

2 Zucchini, sliced
2 Cloves Garlic
1 (16 oz.) Lasagna
1 C. Mixed Vegetables
1 C. Black Olives
2 tsp. Basil

Sauté onion, garlic, and zucchini in ½ cup water. Cook and squeeze water from spinach or use frozen chopped spinach drained. Layer ingredients in an oiled 9X13 inch glass pan, pasta sauce, noodles, tofu cheese, vegetables, olives, and onion mixture. Repeat layers. Top with sauce, olives and parsley. Bake at 350 for 1 hour.

Tofu Cheese

1 lb. Tofu, firm
¼ C. Sesame Tahini
1/3 C. Pimentos
1 tsp. Onion Powder

2 T. Nutritional Yeast
2 T. Lemon Juice, Fresh
1/3 C. Water
½ tsp. Garlic Salt

Combine all ingredients in blender. Blend until smooth. May substitute 1 ½ cup cooked brown rice or corn meal mush for tofu. Ready to use in recipes from blender or you can cook over low heat and thicken with 2 T. cornstarch and 2 T. of cold water blended well and stirred in. Simmer until desired consistency.

Healthy Option Fresh Apple Crisp

6 C. Apples, sliced   ½ tsp. Cinnamon
1 C. Walnuts   ½ C. Raisins
1 tsp. Vanilla   1 C. Dates, pitted
2 T. Lemon Juice   ½ tsp. Nutmeg
½ C. Coconut Flakes   2 T. Honey
½ tsp. Sea Salt   ½ tsp. Sea Salt

Place 1 cup of the sliced apples into a food processor along with the seasonings and blend well. Gently mix blended apple mix with remaining sliced apples and place in a glass pie pan. For topping; blend nuts in food processor add dates, coconut and salt. Sprinkle on top of apples. No need to cook. Refrigerate until ready to serve.

Banana Whipped Cream

½ C. Pineapple Juice   2 Frozen Bananas, sliced
¼ C. Raw Cashews, rinsed   ½ C. Water
4 Dates, pitted   ¼ tsp. Maple Extract

Blend well in blender or food processor and freeze slightly before serving.

www.ChefLindaTrubey.com

DAY 3 RECIPES

Harvest Nut Roast

2 C. Onions, chopped
1 tsp. Basil
2 C. Bread Crumbs
2 T. Oil + ¼ C. Water
1 T. Beef-Style Seasoning

2 C. Pecans, chopped
1 C. Celery, chopped
½ tsp. Sage
1 C. Soy Milk

Sauté onion and celery in oil and water until soft combine all ingredients and mix well. Spray 9X13 pan with olive oil and bake covered at 350 degrees for 45 min. Remove cover and bake 15 min. more.

Chick-Pea Noodle Soup

2 C. Chick-Peas (Garbanzos) broken into thirds
½ C. Onion, chopped fine
½ C. Celery, chopped fine
¼ C. Oil
(optional)

½ lb. Fettuccine Noodles,

2 T. Chicken-Style Seasoning
1 T. Parsley
1 C. Peas & Carrots

In a large soup pan, sauté onions and celery in oil until soft, add 8 cups of water along with remaining ingredients and simmer for 30 minutes. You can add Gluten or Fri-Chick for protein.

Fresh Fruit Salad
2 Apples, Chopped
1 C. Fresh or Frozen Blueberries
1 C. Seedless Grapes
1 C. Banana Slices
1 C. Pineapple Chunks
½ C. Orange Slices
½ C. Shredded Coconut
¼ C. Pineapple or Orange Juice

This recipe makes its own dressing from the pineapple juice and shredded coconut. Mix well and chill until ready to serve.

Roasted Red Pepper Humus
2 C. Chick-Peas (Garbanzos)
1 Clove Garlic
3 T. Lemon Juice
¼ C. Sesame Tahini
½ C. Roasted Red Peppers   ½ tsp. sea salt
½ C. Water   ½ tsp. onion Powder

Rinse and drain peppers, blend all ingredients well in a food processor and chill. Sprinkle paprika and parsley on top. Great as a dip or filling for pita pocket sandwich. You can add sliced olives or green onions. Nutritional Yeast Flakes are another healthy option addition.

DAY 4 RECIPES

Oatmeal Waffles or Pancakes

1 C. Rolled Oats   2 tsp. Honey or Agave
1 C. Water   ½ tsp. Vanilla or Maple Extract
½ Banana   ¼ tsp. Cinnamon
1/8 tsp. Salt   1 T. Flax Seeds, ground

Put ingredients into blender and mix well. Add more water to make waffle batter consistency. For pancakes you can add chopped nuts for extra protein.

Berry Good Fruit Sauce

2 C. Fresh or Frozen Berries
½ C. Apple Juice Concentrate

In a food processor blend 1 cup of the berries with concentrate then gently stir in remaining berries. Great fresh as is or you can thicken with 1 T. Cornstarch and ¼ cup cold water and cook until thickened.

Cashew Whip Cream

1 C. Raw Cashews, rinsed   ½ Orange, fresh juiced
½ tsp. Honey   ¼ tsp. Vanilla
Whip in blender or food processor until smooth add water as necessary to reach a cream consistency and chill.

www.ChefLindaTrubey.com

Nut Meat Balls

1 ½ C. Cornbread Stuffing (Pepperidge Farm)
1 tsp. Basil
1 C. Pecan Meal
½ tsp. Oregano
1/3 C. Parsley, minced
½ tsp. Cumin
1 Sweet Onion, chopped
2 T. Flax Seeds
1 T. Canola Oil + 1 T. Soy Sauce
½ C. Water

Brown the onion and add seasonings. Soak flax seeds in the water, then mix well with the remaining ingredients. Form into balls using 1 Tbsp. measurement, bake at 350 degrees for 25 minutes. These nut meat balls taste great with BBQ Sauce.

Tasty BBQ Sauce

2 T. Olive Oil
1 T. Hickory Flavor
1 Onion, chopped fine
¼ C. Honey BBQ Sauce
1 C. Ketchup
½ C. Brown Sugar

Brown the onion in the oil and cook well. Stir in remaining ingredients and bring to a boil until thick and flavorful.

Black Bean Burgers

2 (15 oz.) Cans Black Beans, rinsed
¼ C. Cilantro, chopped
1 C. Rolled Oats   ¼ C. Applesauce
1 Onion, chopped   ¼ C. Bread Crumbs
1 Clove Garlic, minced   1 T. Olive Oil
2 T. Salsa   1 T. Chili Powder

Mash beans and mix well with oats, onion, garlic, cilantro, salsa, chili powder and applesauce. Form into patties and dip in bread crumbs. Heat oil in skillet and cook on both sides until browned.

Potato Wedges

4 potatoes   1 T. Olive oil
1 tsp. Garlic Powder   ½ tsp. Onion Powder
½ tsp. Rosemary   ½ tsp. Parsley

Peel and cook potatoes, slice into wedges, then cover with oil and seasonings and bake in a 350 degree oven for 10 minutes or until browned. Sprinkle with sea salt to taste.

Healthy Option Carmel Corn

2 C. Popcorn Seeds

1 C. Molasses

½ tsp. Sea Salt

1 C. Peanuts, dry roasted

1 C. Peanut Butter

½ tsp. Cinnamon (optional)

Pop seeds in an air popper ½ cup at a time. In a saucepan stir molasses and peanut butter together, warm to blend well. Place popped corn and peanuts on a baking sheet and drizzle molasses mixture over it and stir until well coated. Add seasonings and bake at 200 degrees for 1 hour until crunchy.

www.ChefLindaTrubey.com

DAY 5 RECIPES

Scrambled Tofu Breakfast Wrap
1 lb. Organic Tofu, drained & rinsed
1 /2 C. Green Onions, chopped
¼ C. Nutritional Yeast Flakes
1 C. Potatoes, cooked & diced
2 tsp. Chicken-Style Seasoning
¼ C. Green Chilies or Bell Pepper
¼ tsp. Garlic Powder
¼ C. Water
½ tsp. Turmeric
½ C. Non-Dairy Cheese

Sauté green onions in the water until the water is evaporated then stir in seasoned tofu and simmer for 10 minutes. Add remaining ingredients and heat well. Serve in whole grain flour tortillas with your favorites like; salsa, olives, guacamole, baco bits, or sausage-style crumbles.

Fresh Salsa

2 Tomatoes	2 Green Onions	1 Garlic Clove
½ C. Cilantro	1 tsp. Cumin	1 tsp. Sea Salt
1 T. Lime Juice	1 T. Olive Oil	Jalapeno to
taste		

Place ingredients into food processor and pulse chop. Allow to sit for a couple of hours for the flavors to blend.

Pecan-Oat Patties

4 C. Oatmeal, cooked
¼ C. Soy Sauce
½ tsp. Garlic Powder
1 C. Pecans, chopped
¼ C. Olive Oil
2 tsp. Onion Powder

Blend well and form into burgers using a ¼ cup scoop. Bake on oiled sheet pan for 30 minutes or fry in pan until nicely browned. For a Garden Burger, just add chopped onions, carrots, and parsley. Experiment with your favorite seasonings and vegetables.

Vegan Gravy

¼ C. Oil or Vegan Margarine
2 T. Beef or Chicken-Style Seasoning
¾ C. Unbleached Flour
2 T. Soy Sauce or Braggs Amino
4 C. Water or Vegetable Broth
1 tsp. Onion Powder

Brown flour in sauce pan, gradually whisk in oil, water, and seasonings. Heat to boiling and simmer until thickened. Poultry seasoning is optional.

Vegan Chick'n Pot Pie   White Sauce

2 C. Fri-Chick or Seasoned Tofu
2 C. Potatoes, cooked   ½ C. Vegan Margarine
1 C. Onions, chopped   ½ C. Unbleached Flour
½ C. Celery, chopped   2 T. Chicken Seasoning
½ C. Carrots, chopped   1 tsp. Garlic Salt
½ C. Green Peas   2 C. Soy Milk

In a large saucepan melt the margarine and stir in the flour.
Cook until bubbly then add warm milk or potato water and
stir until thickened. Season and pour over remaining
ingredients in a 9X13 inch glass pan. Bake at 359 degrees until
bubbly, then top with Quick Crust and bake at 400 degrees
for 8-10 minutes.

Quick Crust

½ C. Warm Water   ½ T. Honey
½ T. Active Dry Yeast   1 tsp. Fine Cornmeal
1 C. Wheat Flour   ½ C. Unbleached Flour

Stir yeast into warm water and honey, add flour and stir.
Place on floured surface and knead for 2 minutes. Roll into
desired shape. For a pizza crust, sprinkle cornmeal on
ungreased pizza pan. Bake at 350 degrees for 20 minutes.

DAY 6 RECIPES

Taco Salad

1 Head of Romaine Lettuce, chopped
½ C. Carrots, grated
½ C. Red or Green Onion, chopped
1 C. Kidney Beans
½ C. Olives, sliced
1 tsp. Taco Seasoning
2 Garden Burgers, crumbled
2 C. Tortilla Chips, crushed

Wash lettuce well and chop fine, mix all ingredients and chill until ready to eat. You can use Ranch salad dressing or tofu sour cream and Fresh Salsa.

Vegan Ranch Dressing

2 C. Veganaise   1 tsp. Dill
1 C. Almond Milk   2 tsp. Parsley
1 T. Honey   2 tsp. Basil
1 T. Lemon Juice   2 tsp. Garlic Powder
2 tsp. Onion Powder   1 tsp. Spike or Herbamare

Whisk until blended well and chill.

Baked Macaroni and Cashew Cheese

1 C. Raw Cashews, rinsed
1 T. Onion Powder
1 tsp. Garlic Powder
½ C. Pimentos or Red Peppers
2 T. Nutritional Yeast Flakes
2 ½ C. Water
3 C. Macaroni, cooked
2 T. Lemon Juice, fresh
2 C. Seasoned Bread Crumbs

Blend all ingredients except ½ cup bread crumbs and the macaroni. Pour sauce over the noodles and bake covered at 350 for 30 minutes. Uncover and sprinkle bread crumbs on top and bake 15 more minutes.

Tropical Smoothie

2 Bananas, Frozen   1 C. Orange Juice, fresh
1 C. Mango, Frozen   1 T. Coconut Flakes

Blend until smooth in a blender. Place paper umbrella and orange slice on glass.

DAY 7 RECIPES

Breakfast Banana Split

1 C. Cooked Oatmeal   ½ C. Crushed Berries
½ C. Crushed Pineapple   2 Bananas, split lengthwise
¼ C. Chopped Walnuts
¼ C. Cashew Whipped Topping

Use a small ice cream scoop for the oatmeal. Place in a bowl and position bananas on each side of cereal. Top with remaining ingredients. Enjoy!

Cashew Whipped Topping

1 C. Raw Cashews, rinsed   ½ Orange, fresh juiced
 ½ tsp. Honey   ¼ tsp. Vanilla

Whip in blender or food processor until smooth add water as necessary to reach a cream consistency and chill or freeze slightly.

Bean Enchiladas

2 C. Refried Beans
1 C. Salsa
4 Corn Tortillas
2 tsp. Paprika
1 tsp. Garlic Salt

Enchilada Sauce

1 T. Canola Oil
2 C. Tomato Sauce
1 C. Tomato Paste
2 tsp. Cumin
2 tsp. Onion Powder

Mix beans and salsa together, spread on a tortilla and roll into enchiladas Place in an oiled baking pan. Mix remaining ingredients to make a sauce and pour on top of enchiladas. Bake at 350 degrees for 30 minutes.

Spanish Rice

4 C. Brown Rice, cooked
½ C. Cilantro or Parsley
1 Onion, chopped fine
1 T. Garlic Salt
½ C. Red & Green Peppers
1 T. Olive Oil
½ C. Celery, chopped fine
1 1/2 C. Tomato Sauce
1 tsp. Paprika
1 tsp. Cumin

Sauté onions, peppers, celery in oil until soft, add rice and sauce with seasonings. Simmer. You can add chopped tomatoes & olives or vegeburger if you like.

Black Bean Soup

1 lb. Black Beans, cooked
½ C. Brown Rice
8 C. Water or vegetable broth
2 C. Mashed Black Beans
1 Red Onion, chopped fine
1 tsp. Chili Powder
1 tsp. Cumin
½ C. Carrots, chopped
½ tsp. Sea Salt
¼ tsp. Cayenne Pepper

Mix well and simmer over low heat. Top with Tofutti sour cream and fresh minced cilantro. Ole'

Tofu Sour Cream

1 lb. Silken Lite Tofu, firm	2 tsp. chopped dill, fresh
1/3 C. Almond Milk	1 T. Nutritional Yeast Flakes
3 T. Fresh Lemon Juice	½ tsp. Sea Salt

Blend until smooth, cover and chill for 1 hour to allow the flavors to blend.

DAY 8 RECIPES

Holiday Nut Roast

1 Onion, chopped

½ C. Soy Milk

1 C. Walnuts, chopped

3 C. Quick Oats

1 (12oz.) Can Vegeburger

1 Clove Garlic, minced

1 T Italian Seasoning

1 lb. Tofu, firm

3 C. Bread Crumbs

1 tsp. Seasoned Salt

Sauté onion and garlic in 1 T. oil or water until browned, blend tofu and soy milk in blender until smooth. Add remaining ingredients and form into a roast. Bake at 350 degrees for 30 minutes then cover top of roast with tomato sauce or ketchup, bake for 30 minutes longer.

Three Bean Chili

2 C. Chili Beans

2 C. Black Beans

2 C. Kidney Beans

2 C. Burger Crumbles

¼ C. Taco Seasoning

4 C. Water

½ C. Green Chilies, diced

4 C. Diced Tomatoes

1 Onion, diced fine

1 T. Canola Oil

2 Cloves Garlic, minced

2 T. Chili Powder

Sauté onion, garlic, burger and taco seasoning in oil, add remaining ingredients and simmer 1 hour. If you like it spicy, add jalapeno peppers.

Tofu Sour Cream

1 lb. Silken Lite Tofu, firm   2 tsp. chopped dill, fresh
1/3 C. Almond Milk   1 T. Nutritional Yeast Flakes
3 T. Fresh Lemon Juice   ½ tsp. Sea Salt

Blend until smooth, cover and chill for 1 hour to allow the flavors to blend.

Coconut Snowball Cookies

½ C. Coconut Oil, melted   ½ C. Honey or Agave
½ C. Cashews, ground   ½ tsp. Vanilla
3 C. Shredded Coconut Flakes (unsweetened)

Blend well and shape into balls, wet hands and roll in coconut flakes. No baking, just keep refrigerated or frozen. You can add chopped nuts or dates for variety. Sometimes I place a whole almond on top and press it down.

DAY 9 RECIPES

Garden Burgers
1 C. Pecans or Walnuts, chopped
½ C. Carrots, grated
2 C. Brown Rice, cooked
1 C. Onion, chopped
1 C. Wheat Bread, torn small
1 T. Oil + 1 T. Water
1 C. Almond or Soy Milk
 ½ tsp. Sage + ½ tsp. Salt

Mix and form into burgers, place on an oiled sheet pan and bake at 350 degrees for 30 minutes or fry in a pan until browned. You can add grated zucchini or chopped bell peppers, celery or any left-over vegetables. If the mixture is too thin, add some ground flax seed to help bind the ingredients together.

Healthy Heart Vegetable Soup
1 ½ C. Onion, chopped
2 C. diced Tomatoes, with juice
1 Clove of Garlic, minced
1 Large Potato, chopped
1 T. Canola Oil
2 C. Vegetable Broth
1C. Celery, chopped
½ C. Parsley, minced
1 C. Carrots, chopped
1 C. Pearl Barley
1 Bay Leaf
1 T. Italian Seasoning

In a large soup pot cook onions and garlic until browned, coarsely chop vegetables and add to soup. Add remaining ingredients and simmer uncovered over low heat. Discard bay leaf. This soup may be prepared ahead of time and frozen.

Fettuccine with Creamy Pesto Sauce

1 ½ C. Fresh Basil	1 ½ C. Fresh Spinach
½ C. Raw Walnuts	¼ C. Pine-nuts
1/3 C. Olive Oil	¼ C. Nutritional Yeast Flakes

1 lb. Fettuccine Noodles or Zucchini Squash for noodles

Prepare fettuccine noodles as directed or make raw noodles from strips of zucchini that you make using a vegetable peeler. Add remaining ingredients to food processor and blend until smooth. You can store in fridge for up to 5 days. Warm and serve.

Peachy Cobbler

½ C. Brown Sugar	½ C. Unbleached Flour
4 C. Peaches with juice	½ C. Vegan Margarine
1 egg replacement	3 T. Minute Tapioca
1 tsp. Vanilla	1 tsp. Cinnamon

Cream sugar and margarine together, add vanilla and egg substitute, then add flour and mix well. Drop by spoonfuls on top of peaches and juice mixed with tapioca and cinnamon in greased baking dish and bake at 350 degrees for 45 minutes then sprinkle cinnamon and sugar on top.

DAY 10 RECIPES

Mock Chicken Salad
½ C. Raw Sunflower Seeds, rinsed
2 Green Onions, sliced
1 C. Raw Cashews, rinsed
½ C. Pecans, chopped
1 Cucumber, peeled & diced
1 Stalk Celery, sliced
½ Lemon, juiced
½ tsp. Dill + ½ tsp. Honey
¼ tsp. Curry Powder
¼ tsp. Sea Salt

Pulse chop seeds and nuts in a food processor until desired consistency, then stir in remaining ingredients and chill until ready to serve. Red grapes sliced in half are pretty and tasty in this salad. Roll up in a collard or lettuce leaf for a raw wrap.

Ranch Dip
1 C. Veganaise
1 C. Tofu Sour Cream
2 tsp. Parsley
2 tsp. Basil
2 tsp. Garlic Powder
1 tsp. Spike or Herbamare
1 tsp. Dill
½ C. Almond Milk
1 T. Honey
1 T. Lemon Juice
2 tsp. Onion Powder

. Whisk until blended well and refrigerate for a couple of hours before serving.

Eggplant Parmesan

1 Eggplant, sliced	1 (10 oz.) Jar Pasta Sauce
½ tsp. Sea Salt	½ tsp. Garlic Powder
1 T. Olive Oil	½ C. Seasoned Bread Crumbs

Peel eggplant and slice into 1/8 inch slices. Put slices in cold water and add salt. Let sit for 10 minutes, then dip soaked slices in bread crumbs mixed with garlic powder. Brown eggplant slices in skillet with olive oil. In a baking dish layer 1/3 of pasta sauce, eggplant slices, sesame parmesan cheese; repeat layers until done. Garnish with fresh parsley and serve with angel hair pasta.

Sesame Parmesan Cheese

¼ C. Sesame Seeds	¼ C. Nutritional Yeast Flakes
2 tsp. Onion Powder	1/3 tsp. Sea Salt
¼ tsp. Garlic Powder	¼ tsp. Basil

Toast sesame seeds in a dry skillet until browned. When cooled mix remaining ingredients well and store in an air tight container.

Italian Salad Dressing

1 C. Olive Oil

2 T. Italian Seasoning

1 tsp. Oregano

½ tsp. Garlic, minced

1 tsp. Sea Salt

½ C. Lemon Juice

½ C. Honey

1 T. Onion Powder

1 tsp. Garlic Powder

Blend together all ingredients until creamy, then store in your refrigerator.

Carob Fudge

1 C. Almond or Peanut Butter

½ C. Chopped Nuts

2 C. Carob Chips

½ C. Raisins or Dates

Place almond butter and carob chips in a sauce pan and stir until melted, add nuts and dates, then spread in a glass pan and refrigerate until firm. Cut into 1 inch squares. This recipe freezes well. Go ahead and make a double batch!

Part 4

Daily Shopping Lists

Day 1 Shopping List

1 head of cabbage

1 green onion

1 green bell pepper

3 cups baby spinach

1 cup broccoli florets

2 bananas

¼ cup shredded coconut

¼ cup pumpkin seeds

½ cup sesame seeds

½ cup honey

¼ cup peanut butter

½ cup millet or brown rice

2 cups brown rice

½ cup sliced almonds

2 cups diced tomatoes

2 cups small white beans

Wheat French bread

2 T. parsley

½ cup olive oil

1 tsp. vanilla

2 onions

4 cloves garlic

1-2 zucchini

1 cup carrots

2 apples

2 lemons

1 cup raw almonds

¼ cup sunflower seeds

¼ cup raisins or cranberries

¼ cup sesame oil

4 cups oatmeal for granola

¼ cup apple juice concentrate

1 lb. tofu, firm

1 cup chow mien noodles

2 cups red kidney beans

½ cup small shell pasta

¼ cup vegan margarine

1 T. Garlic Powder

1 tsp. Italian Seasoning

1 tsp. cinnamon (optional)

Day 2 Shopping List

3 cups spinach

8 apples

½ cup pineapple juice

3 bananas

2 potatoes

2 cloves garlic

2 zucchini

2 tomatoes

1 lemon

2 T. olive oil

2 lbs. tofu, firm

½ cup raisins

1 ½ cup dates

1 cup walnuts

1 cup black olives

1/3 cup pimentos

1 tsp. onion powder

1 romaine lettuce

1 cup pineapple

16 oz. lasagna noodles

26 oz. spaghetti sauce

½ cup green onions

¼ green chilies or bell pepper

¼ cup sesame tahini

8 carrot + celery sticks

¼ cup parsley or cilantro

¾ cup nutritional yeast flakes

2 tsp. chicken-style seasoning

1 cup mixed vegetables

½ tsp. turmeric

½ cup non-dairy cheese

1 tsp. garlic powder

whole grain sub buns

Day 3 Shopping List

4 bananas

2 onions

1 cup celery

2 apples

1 cup grapes

1 orange

1 lemon

1 clove garlic

1 cup walnuts

½ cup dates

1 cup pecans

1/3 cup olive oil

1 T. parsley

½ tsp. sage

sea salt

2-4 potatoes

1 lb. baby carrots

2 cup broccoli

½ cup shredded coconut

1 cup pineapple in 100% juice

1 cup peas & carrots

1 cup blueberries

4 cups garbanzos (chickpeas)

½ cup pimentos or red pepper

3 cups soy or almond milk

2 cups bread crumbs

2 cups rolled oats

2 T. chicken-style seasoning

2 T. beef-style seasoning

½ lb. fettuccine noodles

Day 4 Shopping List

4 apples	2 cups berries (fresh or frozen)
1 onion	2 sweet onions
4 potatoes	2-4 sweet potatoes
2 bananas	½ cup apple juice concentrate
1 orange	¼ cup applesauce
¼ cup olive oil	¼ cup honey BBQ sauce
1 T. honey	2 cups rolled oats
1 tsp. vanilla	1 cup pecan meal
3 T. flax seeds	1 ½ cup cornbread stuffing
1 clove garlic	1/3 cup parsley, fresh
1 cup ketchup	1 cup raw cashews
1 T. hickory flavor	½ cup brown sugar
1 cup frozen peas	4 cups black beans (2 15 oz. cans)
½ cup molasses	1 cup popcorn seeds
½ cup peanut butter	½ cup dry roasted peanuts
1 T. soy sauce	½ tsp. oregano
1 tsp. basil	½ tsp. cumin
2 T. salsa	½ cup cilantro
1 T. chili powder	1 tsp. garlic powder
½ tsp. onion powder	1 tsp. parsley + rosemary

Day 5 Shopping List

4 potatoes

½ green pepper

½ cup celery

½ cup peas

2 tomatoes

1 T. honey

1 cup pecans

2 lbs. tofu, firm

1/3 cup soy sauce

1 cup wheat flour

1 tsp. fine cornmeal

½ T. active dry yeast

1 tsp. garlic powder

Fresh fruit

Trail mix

1 cup green onions

1 cup onion

½ cup carrots

1 clove garlic

1 lime + 1 jalapeno

4 cups oatmeal

¼ cup chicken-style seasoning

½ cup olive oil

1 ½ cups unbleached flour

½ cup cilantro

½ cup non-dairy cheese

3 tsp. onion powder

Sea salt + Cayenne pepper

2 cups soy milk or potato water

½ cup vegan margarine

Day 6 Shopping List

1 red onion	2 heads romaine lettuce
2 tomatoes	4 corn on the cob
1 cup carrots	4 slices whole grain bread
2 oranges	½ cup peanut butter
1 lemon	½ cup pimentos
1 mango	½ cup applesauce
2 bananas	2 T. Nutritional Yeast Flakes
1 cup olives	1 T. coconut oil or flakes
2 garden burgers	1 tsp. taco seasoning
1 cup soy milk	1 cup red kidney beans
1 T. honey	1 cup raw cashews
1 tsp. dill	2 T. onion powder
2 tsp. parsley	1 T. garlic powder
2 tsp. basil	1 tsp. spike seasoning
3 cups macaroni	2 cups seasoned bread crumbs
2 cups veganaise	1 cup salsa
2 granola bars	2-4 cups tortilla chips

www.ChefLindaTrubey.com

Day 7 Shopping List

2 bananas

1 onion

1 red onion

2 cups carrot

1 orange

1 lemon

1 T. garlic salt

1 cup raw cashews

½ cup walnuts

2 cups oatmeal

1 cup salsa

4-6 flour tortillas

1 cup tomato paste

¼ tsp. vanilla

2 T. olive oil

1 T. cumin

¼ cup parsley

2 tsp. dill

2 cups salsa

1 cup humus

2 cups carrots

1 red or green pepper

2½ cup celery

4 whole grain dinner rolls

6 cups black beans

1 cup frozen berries

1 cup crushed pineapple

4 ½ cups brown rice

½ cup soy or almond milk

2 cups refried beans

1 lb tofu (for sour cream)

3 ½ cups tomato sauce

½ tsp. honey

1 tsp. paprika

1 tsp. chili powder

¼ cup cilantro

1 T. nutritional yeast flakes

sea salt + cayenne pepper

6 cups tortilla chips

Day 8 Shopping List

2 apples

2 oranges

1 lemon

3 cloves garlic

1 cup walnuts

2 onions

½ cup dates

½ cup honey

1 lb. tofu

2 cups chili beans

2 cups black beans

2 cups kidney beans

3 cups quick oats

1 cup soy milk

½ tsp. vanilla

2 tsp. dill

½ cup coconut oil

1 cup seven grain cereal

4 cups diced tomatoes

1 head green leafy lettuce

2 cups baby spinach

3 cups shredded coconut

½ cup raw cashews

¼ cup green chilies, diced

2(19 oz.) cans vege-burger

3 cups seasoned bread crumbs

2-4 cups mashed potatoes

¼ cup taco seasoning

1 T. canola oil

2 T. chili powder

1 T. nutritional yeast

1 tsp. seasoned salt

½ cup tofu sour cream

sea salt + cayenne pepper

Day 9 Shopping List

1 romaine lettuce

2 tomatoes

2 cups carrots

Melons (variety)

1 cup celery

1 ½ cup fresh basil

2 cups fresh spinach

½ cup fresh parsley

2 ½ cup onions

2 potatoes

1 clove garlic

½ cup olive oil

1 cup soy milk

1 tsp. sugar

½ cup pine nuts

1 tsp. vanilla

¼ cup pickles

Ketchup

1 ½ cup pecans or walnuts

2 cups vegetable broth

2 cups diced tomatoes

4 cups peaches with juice

1 cup pearl barley

2 cups brown rice

½ cup unbleached flour

1 cup wheat bread cubes

½ cup vegan margarine

¼ cup nutritional yeast flakes

1 T. Italian seasoning

3 T. minute tapioca

1 tsp. cinnamon

1 egg replacement

½ tsp. sage

1 bay leaf

2-4 wheat burger buns

1 lb. (16 oz.) fettuccine noodles

Day 10 Shopping List

1 eggplant	½ cup raw sunflower seeds
2 green onions	¼ cup sesame seeds
1 clove garlic	1 cup pecans
2 cups celery	2 cups granola
Romaine lettuce	4 cups almond milk
2 carrots	1 cup veganaise
2 grapefruit	1 cup tofu sour cream
3 lemons	1 jar (28 oz.) spaghetti sauce
1 cucumber	6 mandarin oranges
1/3 cup honey	½ cup seasoned bread crumbs
1 ½ tsp. dill	½ cup sliced almonds
2 cups carob chips	1 cup peanut or almond butter
½ cup raisins	¼ cup nutritional yeast flakes
1 T. basil	¼ tsp. curry powder
1 cup olive oil	3 T. onion powder
1 tsp. oregano	2 T. garlic powder
1 tsp. spike	2 T. Italian seasoning
Sea salt	

Pass It On   Lyrics by Kurt Kaiser

It only takes a spark to get a fire going.
And soon all those around can warm up in its glowing.
That's how it is with God's love,
Once you've experience it.
You spread his love to everyone;
You want to pass it on.

What a wondrous time is spring,
When all the trees are budding
The birds begin to sing, the flowers start their
blooming;
That's how it is with God's love,
Once you've experienced it.
You want to sing, it's fresh like spring,
You want to pass it on.

I wish for you my friend, this happiness that I've found;
you can depend on him, it matters not where you're
bound.
I'll shout it from the mountaintop;
I want my world to know;
the Lord of love has come to me,
I want to pass it on."

www.ChefLindaTrubey.com

Go Light Your World   Lyrics by Chris Rice

There is a candle in every soul
Some brightly burning, some dark and cold
There is a spirit who brings a fire
Ignites a candle, and makes his home

Carry your candle
Run to the darkness
Seek out the helpless, confused and torn
And hold out your candle
For all to see it
Take your candle and go light your world

Frustrated brother, see how he's tried to
Light his own candle some other way
See now your sister she's been robbed and lied to
Still holds a candle, without a flame

Carry your candle
Run to the darkness
Seek out the lonely, the tired and worn
And hold out your candle
For all to see it
Take your candle and go light your world
Take your candle and go light your world

Cuz we are a family
Whose hearts are blazing
So lets raise our candles and light up the sky
Prayin to our Father in the name of Jesus
Make us a beacon in darkest times

Carry your candle
Run to the darkness
Seek out the hopeless, deceived and
Hold out your candle
For all to see it